Vibrant Eons

101 Poems About The Light, The Dark, And Somewhere In Between

By David Coad

Published by Lyvit Publishing, Cornwall

www.lyvit.com

ISBN 978-0-9555061-2-3

Dedicated to my Fiancée, Clare:

She cares,

She understands,

She comforts,

She gives,

She loves.

The Author would like to thank the following in the making of this book:

Sarah Peters, for her wonderful cover pictures;
Terry Lander and his wife, **Mary**, for their time in printing and publishing this book;
Richie Lemon, for giving me that push;
Ben Nicholls, for his wisdom.

Love and thanks to:

Clare Hillier, my Fiancée, for putting up with me. I love you so much;
Mum and **Dad**, for looking after me for far too many years;
Simon McKeown, my best friend for over 20 years. It's about time you visited us in your Tardis;
Sarah Peters, my best lady, artist and friend. Party On!
Richie and **Nina Lemon**, for their friendship, love, and meadwine;
Kevin and **Carol Jenkins**, for their friendship, love, and meadwine;
Neil, **Tracey** and **Amy**, for their love, help and guidance;
Bob and **Sylvia**, for their love, understanding and wisdom;
Peter and **Sue Critchinson**, for giving me a chance. Thank you;
Donna Game, for her friendship and cutting my hair;
Richard and **Colleen**, for their love;
Sue, **Sarah**, **Joanne** and **Jack**, love and kisses;
Daniel and **Jo Roy**, for their support;
Aunty Maud and **Aunty Helen**, love and thanks.

Indirect thanks to:

Pink Floyd, Radiohead, Fleetwood Mac, Katherine Jenkins, Kylie Minogue, JRR Tolkien, George Orwell, Ian Fleming, James Herbert, Stephen King, Shaun Hutson, William Horwood, LucasArts, Valve, Melbourne House, Arsenal FC and lastly Neighbours.

Contents

Contents

Contents

"Life is a book. Every day we turn another page in that book. We never know where this new day, this new page, will take us. Yet whether it's glowing in light or surrounded by darkness, turn, walk, breathe, live."

David Coad, 7th November 2006

Different Light

A river, strawberry light
The suns rays, moonbeam sight
Colours cast, paints a scene
Inside a rainbow, inside a dream
Cast a light on pale shade
A different angle colour made
Spectrum eyes, seas of green
Dripping paintbrush, setting the scene
Stars in space, candle-light
The darkness before dawn, twilight
In the distance a semi-glow
The Shepherds in the shadows, we follow
Deep in Heavens, the sun and the moon set ablaze
Aimlessly wandering through the haze
Melting moon, earth rips
Spectacular sun, solar eclipse.

Pocket Of Frost

Pocket of frost
Cool morning breeze
Surrounded by fog
In fire we freeze.

Pocket of frost
Sap turned to ice
Glisten of the icicle
Snowflake to spice.

Pocket of frost
Shake and shiver
Deep frozen lake
Long twisting river.

Pocket of frost
Never to leave
Crisp clean air
In life we breathe.

The Bluebell Wood

Untouched by man, hidden from view
The bluebell wood, through ages it grew
Populated by animal, insect, and bird
The living of nature, the only sound to be heard.

Splashes of colour, clustered in May
The scent of nectar, it wafts away
A sight to behold, rooted in the soil
The bees spoilt for choice, endlessly they toil.

Mysterious and haunting, we tread the path
Respectful of nature, we play and laugh
Deep into it's arms, we wonder and gaze
Lying in deep grass, under the summer sky we laze.

Through autumn, winter, summer, and spring
Its appeal undiminished, birds chorus sing
The bluebell wood, our secret haven
Where we become one, with nature.

Leopard Mine

Touch of mink, stroke of fur
Feel what once did purr
Fish of the lake, fish of the river
Fish, fry and gently simmer
Dolphin in the net, whale by the spear
Tough meat for dinner washed down with a beer
Red cloak and dagger, bull in the ring
Matador bows in the arena, crowds sing
Flap of the pheasant, paddle of the duck
Avoiding a hail of bullets, with any luck
Growl of the wolf, roar of the bear
Measured to fit, warm to wear
Leopard can sprint, leopard can run
Leopard can't out-run a bullet from a gun
Tail holds trunk, waterhole by dusk
Dead by dawn for an ivory tusk
When there's nothing left to hunt and nothing left to kill
Man will have to answer and pay a heavy bill
Man will hunt man for the ultimate thrill
When man has wiped out man, man will have paid the bill!

A Blank Piece Of Paper

This was a blank piece of paper
Destined for nothing
Destined for a bin
But now I shall paint such words on its canvass
Illuminating such pictures, such music, such poetry
So many scenes by the setting of words
To invent a taste by the bleeding of my ink
On this piece of paper that was blank, dead, lifeless
I give you life to light, I give you pictures painted
Photographs in the beads of your eyes
Dreams in the depths of your mind
A story to tell on my blank piece of paper
So my friends prepare yourselves for all the colours bar blank
And it goes something like this...

The Greatest Day Of My Life

To Clare Hillier.

The greatest day of my life was yesterday
For yesterday I met Clare
And from the very moment I met her
My life would never be the same again.

To fall so utterly in love with someone
To want to be with them all the hours in the day
All the days of the week
All the weeks of the month
All the months of the year
And all the years to come
For everyday is the greatest day of my life
Because I'm with Clare
Yet no matter how great today is
There is always tomorrow
Which becomes the greatest day of my life.

Missing Olds

They're over there, and I'm over here,
Remembering how it used to be,
Fire in the sun and the folds of the fields,
Green on green, seen and unseen,
Fields that flowed into forests,
Streams that tumbled over meadows,
Part of my life, part of my dream,
My dream seen and unseen.

Now I'm living in a concrete jungle,
And what was once mine I miss so,
Where the green is unseen,
Where there is noise and filth,
Where the air is unclean, unseen,
Where I long for days of olds,
Where the people here seem unfriendly, alien,
For the love of one I sacrifice everything,
Where I dream of clean and green.

The Day and Us

There is only the day and us
Today we grabbed it and lived it
And so we journeyed hand in hand
On the sea, over land
We laughed in the sun and we drank in the rain
We rolled over and over in fields of green
Under colour, over shadow
Out of light our minds sight
Today was born of us
And in our light we passed.

Glitter Bay

To Hayle beach in Cornwall.

There is a beach where I live, and I call it Glitter Bay
For it is truly blessed, a jewel in our haven
Formed eons ago by the hand of promise
Sacred, tranquil, lush in smooth layers of sultry sand
And inside its outer beauty; a pearl
A sea as blue as the clear sky
A sun rides it's booming waves over an ocean
To lap at our feet in the joys of summer
Where families flock, where surfers surf
To walk, to run, to play, to look, to bathe
And when in winter's bitter hours
Alone it endures in glittering tranquility
For all the promises born, for all the promise of joy
All your summers still to come
All your walks and laughter
It holds them all in it's salty breath
Beneath it's soft silky sand
An arena for you.

Behold Batman

I am the darkness, I am the night,
I am revenge, I am the right.

I am fear, I am sleuth,
I am vengeance, I am the truth.

I am justice, I am wrath,
I am a freak, a tortured behemoth.

I am horror, I am alone,
I am forever shadow, on a moonlight throne.

Behold the night, behold the moon,
Behold Batman, thy living rune!

Fantasy Land

Come with me now to a place in time
Where the taverns were full, with music and rhyme
The king in his castle, the queen by his side
Their kingdom vast, with horses to ride.

Wizards and warriors, magical and brave
Trade across the ocean, on the crest of a wave
Princes and princesses, fair and wise
Dragons in the mountains, breathing fire he flies.

Damsels in distress, locked up high in a tower
A knight in shining armour, he shall not cower
To find the hidden treasure, who will take thy quest
Many creatures to slay, and her hand for any who pass the test.

Swords and sorcery, traitors and a witch
Smugglers and bandits, hiding in a ditch
A large dark forest, a quiet placid lake,
Fantasy land, my lovely dream, but now it's time to wake.

Victory Roll

In an awesome display of speed and power
The victor guided his fighter back over the cheering citizens
A low deafening roar of victory
Doing a victory roll in his exaltation and overflowing adrenalin rush
As his vanquished enemies burned and melted in their ruin
His fighter blazing away into the distance
As open-mouthed people look up in wonder
At their saviour, at their angel of death
Understanding in their joy that destruction is beautiful
Menace has an art
Fear is an advantage
As smoke billows from the fiery mangled wreckage of their foes
Their pyre is his ecstasy
Boys want to be him
Girls want to marry him
He only lives for the clouds
And that searing speed.

Daydream Inside

When I am sitting, surveying the scene
I seem to dream
I float away on the breath of the wind
Endlessly streaming over hills of this land
Where once I trod on days gone by
When things were different in younger days
Where I was young, where I was born
But now I am old, age long worn
I wonder when and where and why
But it gets me nowhere
So I dream away the day
To places not yet born
Yet born to my sight
My everlasting light
In these darker days beneath the storm
Where clouds gather and brood
Awaking me to their angry mood
By clap of thunder, flash of fire
Inside my dream, evergreen
Over rivers streaming overflow
Rolling into paradise gleaming
Inside, is this feeling.

There Are No Superheroes

For September 11th, 2001.

The world turned away
The fires burned bright
The people wept in despair
The shocking stood and stared
There are no happy days
There are no family values
For the storms that batter our homes
Wear us down to a new level.

For those who knew the pain
The lost who forever wander
Is this the price we pay
For the way we live and die?
Why didn't somebody do something?
Where were the superheros?
There are no superheroes
Just mortal heroes
Who live and die.

The Loneliest Face

The loneliest face in the world
Is the one who stares back at you
When you look in the mirror
Trapped forever in its prison
To be eternally looking out
Always there when you look in
Never to be released
That's the loneliest face.

Some Days

Some days it's there
Some days it's not there
I can't explain it
I only know that some days I have the power
And when I have the power, it's so strong
I can create anything with my words
My mind's a never-ending explosion of ideas and themes
Images and designs that wrap around my feelings
I see distant worlds, colourful collages, and erotic poses
I weep with despair and tragedy on a grand scale
I rejoice with epic pleasure for the sacred bounty of true love
On days like these, I have such power
And other days, there is nothing
Just nothing.

A Farewell To Friends

We don't see them coming
We never see them go
How they come into our lives
Then leave without a trace
Just a distant memory
Cant remember their face
Forgotten their names
All our friends of yesterdays
Gone to horizons lost.

They touch our lives for a brief instance
Leaving us with sight and sound
For we all wander cold and lost
Until a friend is found
A friendly face from now, from then
Always moving on
I hear their echoes across the land
A distant goodbye, farewell.

All That You Left Behind

For my friend, Sarah Peters

An end of an era marks this day
Between the sun and the moon
Many goodbyes, wheres and whys
Paths to places where your welcome slowly wore
Gazing at distant horizons for adventure and so much more
Such a wrench to uproot the youth of old
Being scared, being brave, being bold
For one so young a story still to unfold
A legacy yet untold
Wandering lonely into the unknown
Where others before and after have flown
Grasping hopes and dreams
Inside your heart where it ever gleams
Forward is the darkness, forward is the light
Forward is your future, shining ever bright.

Movement

To be moved
Nothing else matters
But to be moved
In mind, in body and in spirit
To take you to a higher place
And be moved
By image, by touch, by the feelings that draw you ever in
To rise up for the briefest of moments above everyone and
everything
And be moved
By the touch of your lover
By the tears flooding down your face
By the shattering climax of sex
By the loss of a loved one
By the birth of life
By the one who cuddles you
For the relief of the weekend
For the one you help
For the injured animal you saved
For the fires burning in your soul
For the stamina in your spirit
For the despair in your grief
For the power of love
For the tranquil countryside
For the boom of the surf
For the pleasure in revenge
For the timid fox, risking a feed in your back garden
For the ring on your finger
For the freedom of the open road
For the exhilaration in speed
For the wild untamed wind that ever feeds our breath
By our actions and the actions of all life
There is movement.
To be moved
Nothing else matters.

Dinner on the Beach

After a long hot summer's day
With food and drink prepared
I invite my love for dinner on the beach with me.

The evening embraced us with its cooling salty sea air
As children's sandcastles slowly melted back into sand
Under the oncoming turn of the tide
Seagulls swooped and swayed over and under waves
Sailing boats gliding up and down
Surfers surfing, and falling
People walking dogs, throwing sticks for them to chase
Families playing the final over of their beach cricket
As the evening slowly drapes it's darkening canvas across the
sky.

We sit on our tartan picnic rug and talk away our day
Above us the sinking sun joins in unison with the sky
Painting a rich canvas of glittering gold, cosmic blushing red
A crimson dream on a numbing purple haze
Under which we ate and drank the night away
A swirling of emotion
The touch of love
Glowing, under the stars.

Buds

To the Spring.

They herald the oncoming of spring
Born from the decay of last autumn
Slowly they ripen, through wind, rain, ice, and snow
Encased, protected and warm in a fruitful skin
Battered by the weather
As time swings around again
The sun is the magical spark
Warmth and soft rain
As the seasons turn full circle
Buds everywhere open to life
Our reward is their colourful displays
An invitation to the bees and insects to drink
So raise your glasses of nectar
And sing, for it is at last, spring.

Hearts Go

Curls and curves where fragrance swirls
Handsome men mingle with pretty girls
How you step and how you swim
Strangers all around you, overflowing from the brim
A single glance is all it took
From you to them, the earth shook
All the hearts you set aglow
Eyes transfixed, follow
Hearts rip eternal at a searing pound
Hearts go hurling through you, shattering into the ground.

Hormones dancing from the hearts of the wise
Rising lust, melting from all those eyes
You look away, moving on with your day
They remain paralyzed, transfixed, floating away
The bittersweet undoing of every man
To fall utterly in love with this woman
She's walking away, starting to fade
All those men, none get saved
Hearts go flying at a deafening sound
Hearts go dying with a tragic pound
All those girls all those curls, never to be seen again
All those curves, all those swirls, oh the pain
Hearts go lightning, crying out in despair
Hearts go vapour trails, at beauty so rare
Hearts go thunder at such loss of love
Hearts go lightspeed to Heaven above.

A Season's Surprise

With the sun rising up, beyond the dawn mist
Summer greetings, for we have all been kissed
Sea-blue sky, flows to horizons lost
Melting the land, soaked in frost
I slip and slide where others glide
Away we fade, into the shade
As the sun rides high, inside outer sky
Its warming cool soothes, our daily cruise
Long afternoon slumber, in the garden of delight
Nature paints a rainbow, which arcs at a dazzling height
Colours drip and run in a shower of shimmering rain
Round and round it squeaks and turns, our rusty weather vane
A seasons surprise today for nature played a magical part
As night surrounds us and lays us down, left to dream, nature's art.

Cherry Red Flake White

To the wonder of Christmas.

Snow falls
Creating a magical world of white
Gripped in the frenzy of Christmas
Glitter and tinsel
A tree draped in colour and light
Reflecting the joy of children
And the hopes of adults.

A robin hops
Church bells ring
Carol singers light the way
For tonight a torch burns high in the Heavens
A single star burns brightest
And it touches every living heart
Filling all things with light, joy, and love
It never fades and it never dies
For now is the birth
Now is the celebration
Reflected in lands far and wide
All joining together in harmony
In the gift of Christmas.

Away From You

How you crawl by hours, away from you
Such a cruel crawl
Pondering on the passings that have been and gone
Those moments that live on in my future, your past
Lonely are the moments with you, after you're gone
Such a wrench that tears at the soul
Remembering our times together and how they were
Such a cruel crawl
Just a blind haze surrounding you
Still I bleed in my heart's belief of you
Trusting that one day you will come
You won't stop coming
Coming and going like we should
A bit like I do now, alone, with the image of you
Till then, it'll be a cruel crawl
Away from you
A cruel, cruel crawl.

The Huddled Masses

For those who perished in the trenches in World War 1.

The huddled masses
Awake they sleep, asleep they wake
In this hour it's all one can take
A numbed body, too fit to die
Too scared to laugh, too proud to cry.

Over the top lies a vast plain
And weary enemy too vicious to tame
Give me my life or give me my death
I've got no stomach to wait here with my freezing breath.

Friend Of The Rebellion

We walk hand in hand in victory
A glorious feeling inside us
As the victors of the bloodiest battle yet
The one that claimed the most
For all about us is glorious ruin
Our town that once we loved, now a smouldering ruin
All around us are broken buildings
Smashed masonry and endless fires
Belching thick choking black smoke drifting into a darkening sky
The eerie cries of the dying
Distant barks from scavenging dogs
Lost children stumble, crying out for dead loved ones
And the discarded weapons of the fallen lie where they fell
Yes, my friend, it is our victory to savour
And what a prize...RUIN!
Once a proud town. Now just a shocking truth
A friend of the rebellion, I have lost forever.

Alien Earth

To mother earth. I wish more people looked after her.

A ruined man beats his fists in frustration
A raped prostitute lies in the gutter, bleeding
An abused child shakes in her room in terror
An old lady shivers in her living room in deepest winter
An abandoned dog wanders lonely streets, starving
The unemployed and homeless gaze into shop windows in awe
Young men cut down in their prime, die in the mud, all for the lines
on a map
Nations plot their neighbours' annihilation with mushroom clouds
Half this planet starve, while the other half pretend not to notice,
gorging themselves.
Wildlife driven to extinction
Tears flood oceans, blood drenches land
Living in fear all the days of your life
And the name of this Hell? This inhuman planet?
EARTH!
A better place not yet born
A legacy stained by the alien in us all.

Old Ace

I still remember now
As if it were a dream
The living breathing legend
I'd swear I'd never seen.

Now a rusting shell
Twisting metal and steel
Dust covers many images
Showing how many it did kill.

Sun gleams on it's body
Crowds did cheer and sing
The home-coming of the ace
In the skies it reined king.

Memories of days long gone
Thoughts of yesteryears
Silent it waits forever
Crying drips of oil tears.

Grains Of Sand

Her siren's voice called out to me
Her song of love of what will be
We walked along the beach, hand in hand
The boom of the surf, silk of the sand
Staring into each other's eyes of love
Just us, the night, and the stars above
Two souls collide in the salty air
As we kissed on the edge of the earth, not a care
I stroked her hair, so long so fair
I kissed her lips and felt heart-strings rip
And with the rising of the tide
We held each other in bliss and died
Floating away, far, far away
Boy and girl, so all our yesterdays will be today
Grains of sand you will be
Forever you, forever me.

Nightmaids

The night has a thousand eyes all gazing at you
Blind between the darkness
They see you on your way
Guiding by the stars, shining by the moon
They all look on you
Sisters of the night
Ghosts in tune with the dream of the unfolding night
Rapture in their vapour
Silent silk flutters from ancient decay
An endless silent cry
Out there in the dark, they cry on you
They guide you home to safety
Yet they can take you, guide you into nowhere
Where you will be lost to mortals
Taken, like they were, to marshal the night
To guide, to capture, mortal sight.

Moments Of Destiny

In every second of time a mortal is blessed
A fate sealed by an invisible host
From a power beyond
Signifying a moment of destiny by which life is lived
To a day, to an hour, to a lifetime
So your past has meaning, your future…belongs
Others will join, others will give, others will love
And so the circle goes
From birth to death, born again
Where makers meet the reborn
Souls set ablaze from Heaven's sight
A dream to live as one
To do great things
To enrich the lives of all you meet
To bring knowledge and understanding
Hope and love
To do what's right and to help one another
To join as one in friendship
My life, a life, any life
From beyond, touched in a second, every second.

Sunstar

There's darkness ahead by the side of the moon
The sun and the stars looked on in tune
Eclipsed by daybreak in high summer June
The sky sank blood-red for tomorrow, too soon.

I gazed for hours at the sky at night
An understanding of silence at an impossible height
A shooting star seers across the Heavens, trails brilliant light
Take your bow beautiful darkness, as you take to flight.

Creatures of the night your time has come
Awake from under night's blanket, undo what you have done
Stalking in the shadows, your menace has begun
As we join forces with the darkness, and walk as one.

Rays of pure light rain down at the birth of dawn
From the womb of Mother Nature, night is mercilessly torn
The battle between day and night, we cower beneath the storm
Darkness, light, day and night, born to be reborn.

The Blackberry

To England's Beautiful Wild Countryside.

From green to red then black
Through rain and sunshine
Through summer into autumn
There it sits and waits
For a grabbing hand
For a hungry mouth
Just a mouthful of goodness
That is the English countryside
Waiting with all it's family tree
Buried amongst the brambles
The prickly thrones and stinging nettles
Waiting to become one of many in a pie
Or a precious gift to a wandering mouse
A tasty snack for a hungry bird
But whatever its fate
It is forever England's autumn countryside;
The humble blackberry.

Holiday Forever

A holiday from home
Where no one knows your name
You come and you go
And you always look the same
The heat of the day
The cool of the night
Sparkle in the sun
Dance under moonlight
Promise of the east
Bounty of the west
To escape my north
To the south my rest
Where love is forever blessed
Where the days never end
To live in permanent bliss
Where time is forever your friend.

Just Another Birthday

Just another birthday, my birthday
That special day, special for me
But as the years roll by, who remembers? Who cares?

Jelly and ice cream, presents and cards, a cake with candles
Those days are gone
What once meant so much, now means an empty doormat
And a glance back to yesterday's memories.

Do they still remember? Do they still care?
Do I remember their birthdays?
No! They are all long gone, far, far away.

Birthdays are the days of youth
It is only when you get older, that you realize
It's just another day
My birthday.

Odd One Out

How they looked and how they stare
At what you are and what you wear
Fingers that point, tongues that taunt
As you hide in the darkness where memories haunt
Nowhere to turn, nowhere to run
You're always miserable, they're always having fun
The wrong clothes, the wrong hair
But you looked beyond, you really didn't care
For the light shined on you, and you strayed from the sheep
And now the individual will sow what you reap
One day they will know, one day they will see
That deep within their souls, they lost their heart's key.

It's Up For Grabs Now

*To Arsenal Football Club for May 1989 & ITV Commentator Brian
Moore.*

One second of utter disbelief
Where all your dreams and aspirations come true
Where time stops
Where time and reality have no meaning, no life
Just the feeling of pure joy
In a hazy blur of timeless slow motion
A numb moment
Where all your orgasms pinnacle into the dream
The dream that becomes reality
Reality that sucks you back
Dazed in a beautiful moment
Captured in a split second of life
Living the dream
The beautiful game.

The Extraordinary Ordinary

It is a beautiful scene, seen through ordinary eyes
That which you cast your sight upon;
Dawn breaking on the horizon
The stars twinkling in the night sky
Rolling fields in the summer sun
Raindrops racing down the window
Snowflakes gliding onto a land of white
Flowers gently swaying in full bloom
A child's sweet smile
A lonely tear rolling down the cheek of the sad
The grace of a female
The strength of a male
The power of an engine
The flames of the fire
The waves of the wild sea
The clouds in the sky
A love eternal
Seen through the eyes of the ordinary
Gasp at the extraordinary.

Live For Today

Breathe in the air
So fresh, so fair
And live for today
In work and play
Smile and cheer
Love, and hold dear
For tomorrow will come
When your day is done.

My Words I Wrote

My words that this day I wrote
And I die
But the words remain
My family die
But the words remain
My generation dies
But the words remain
The earth dies
But the words remain
Mankind dies
But the words remain
The universe dies
But the words remain
Time ceases
But the words remain
Eternally engraved in space, timeless
For the words were once, written.

Mountain Side

To all the people who have touched me in my life.

Age-long I have dwelt
Weather beaten through seasons long;
Long hot sultry summers
Through falling leaves of autumns wane
The shiver and glittering white of winter's bite
The glory and bloom of the spring.

My peak reaches far up past Heaven
My roots twist and turn all the way down to Hell
Yet here I stand, unmovable, untouchable
A rock to be leaned on when you need me
My hands to lift you when you fall
My friendship to keep close in your heart
My love to feel all the days of your life.

Each and every person that touches me is a miracle
Each and every person takes a chunk out of me
Cracks are in me everywhere
Cracks that shape me into the mountain that I am
For I am age-long
My love immortal
My heart everlasting
So please lean on me, my mountain side
Whenever you need a friend
I am going nowhere
For my love is everywhere
Inside this mountain my heart beats for you.

The Sound Of The Sea

To my Fiancée, Clare.

As the early morning mist melted away
We walked along the coastal path to the special place where I did pray
Overlooking Lamorna Cove, where all could see
Bravely I knelt down on one knee
The white gold diamond ring sparkled it's magic light
Time stopped for David and Clare, a moment of pure sight
With the angels of love blessing us beyond the sound of the sea
I asked my love to marry me
A monumental moment sealed in our time
Together we wept with joy, yours is mine
Our love glowing from our souls, from our hearts
Where boyfriend's and girlfriend's journeys end, fiancée's journey starts
Our faith, our trust, bound by a single kiss
Beyond this moment of our engagement, lay our eternal bliss.

Bliss In Sleep

To Clare.

Breathless, takes a life from me
Lying next to you
So soft, so peaceful, in sleep
I bathe in ripples of silk
Touching your spirit
Gliding through hours uncounted
Watching over you
At bliss in sleep
Dream away thy love
Silent hours comfort me
Listening to your soft breath of life
Into and beyond the dead of night
As I slowly slip, drifting under
Joining with you
On the edge of dreams
Till the dawn chorus wakes us.

Night Lake

Moonbeams reflect off sunlit dreams
A heavy dew flows
Tall reeds glint and sway in the dawn breeze
All the lake shivers in silver shadows
A breathless place, deep within
A ghost floating on the water
Searching for something she lost long ago
Weeping ripples of tears into the night lake
Rising sun, she begins to fade
Beneath the lake, drowning days
Numb cold water where they freeze
Waiting for the night, to weep
For her folly of once being young, wild, and free
To this lake she is forever chained
To search in vain for her lost, every night

Lady Snake

Entombed under the light, darkness stirs
She rises out of the pool
Cool water trickles off her glistening skin
Eyes closed, she breathes in the moist cave air
Holding up her arms, dancing out of the pool, she cools
Clouds of vapour rise from her hot steaming body, alerting snakes
They slither along their tunnels to the pool
There they rise and fall in motion with her
Mistress and servant in perfect symmetry
Her soaking blonde hair, lighting up the cave
Its colours coming to the forefront
Deathly it sounds with the hiss and slither of ancient evil
Poison rises from its cracks like winter frost
Carvings etched into the rock from the dead
Forgotten ceremonies of fire and water; sacrifice into enlightenment
Her fingers read the words of her fore-fathers, her victims, her
children
Snakes glide twisting, tantalizing up her shapely legs
Winding round and round and round and up
Quivering, all snakes suddenly stop dead
They slither round and round and round and down
There they stare at their mistress
Her eyelids lift open to show blazing black eyes
Leaving all naked to her mercy
All are paralyzed at Lady Snake
Tombs tremble above and below at her ghost
She writhes in the rhythm of life, new life
Shedding her old skin for this new form
Licked clean by her children, her slaves
Dancing for the memory, for existence, for rule absolute
Her dancing tongue lashes out, laced with deadly poison
For life beyond.

Falling Star

Star of light, streaking across the sky
Feeling so alive, such a freedom to fly
Searing across the Heavens, blazing beautiful and bright
For all to gasp at as they gaze in wonder long into the night.

Shattering past mountains, the far and the wide
Reflections over oceans moving with their tide
Such a perfect ride under the shining moon
About to come to my end, all too soon.

Collision course, crashing into earth
My death is my sacrifice for a new birth
People stare at my fading light, wondering why
For every new birth, a star must die.

My vapour trails float like a cloud
The star that was me, a child so proud
Child's tearful eyes looking up at the sky
Wondering why, one day we have to die.

Autumn Falls

A shivered whisper from beyond calls
So long summer, autumn falls
Echoes dancing in the mist
Seasonal turnings, turnings twist
The burnt and broken laid to rest
As we gaze at the Shepherd's sky going down in the west
Horizons colour heralds change
Gardeners turn over the next leaf, next page
Earthy damp, chilling to the bone
Roaring fire to welcome you home
The leaves are falling from the sky at night
As we all look up in wonder at frozen light
Huddled together for a coming Halloween
Its summers long lost sister; autumn, the dark queen!

The Girl With A Bow In Her Hair

The girl with a bow in her hair
Sitting behind the haystack
Under the midday sun
In the cornfield
By the farm
Daydreaming about being in love with a dashing handsome man
Who would take her away from this dull place
Into a city full of lights, splendour, and excitement
Where she would come out of herself and die in his arms
And he would wine and dine her
Shower her with jewels and diamonds
Dress her in the finest gowns and dresses
Take her here, there and everywhere in his sleek shiny flash sports car
Introduce her to all his friends
Live in his luxury penthouse where they would kiss and make love
Be waited on by servants and have everything at the click of her fingers
And she would become a beautiful glamorous lady
And he would be a...

Suddenly she was snapped out of her daydream and back to reality by her father shouting at her,
"THAT HAY MUST BE STACKED BY SUNDOWN! DO YOU HEAR ME, GIRL?"
Oh, to dream and to want and to wish; to live
She thought as she picked up her fork and got back to her work.

Sunday In England

Sunday in England
Set in time
Fields that lay you down
Beaches that lap at your toes
Lawnmowers whirr in melody
A family gathering roast
Newspapers that take a week to read
A grand prix fit for the settee
A ploughman's at the pub
A slow snaking drive in the countryside
Long summer snooze on a sunny lazy Sunday
Set in time
Sunday in England.

Foxes Field

For nature's wildlife everywhere.

These fields of green that flow and sway
Embracing shadows far away
For what we see and what we believe
Gives us life and makes us breathe.

The long lush green grass of summer
Holds within it's forest, many a miracle
The youth of life and the breath of air
Carried on the wind, nature's prayer.

The big brown eyes of a devoted mother looks on
As she watches over her fox cubs playing in the field
Jumping and rolling and play-fighting in the long lush green grass
Such innocence in the youth of life
Such wondrous spirit and play in the arms of nature
For the joy of brother and sister
Within these fields their days grow old.

Oblivious to danger and the evils of mankind
Youth plays on
A moment of priceless life
Beyond all glittering gold
Today, where green fields beckoned
Cubs that came to play
Dancing and jumping in playful bliss
For moments in memories days.

Seen by my eyes, and leaving me stunned
Such is the power of nature
I thank her for allowing me to witness this miracle
Within her kingdom, her earth.

Spirit Of Life

Spirit of life in young eyes, wonder
So much time to live, breathe, dance
Fly wild spirit to wherever, whenever
On the wings of breath you dazzle under the sun
Under shadows pale banner you shiver in the breeze
Silent sleep beneath twilight
Taking the hand of dawns still waters
Where you gently float away
Like a mist that never was
A dream that faded away
Leaving nothing, save memory, save wonder.

The Man With No Name

Again I fall to the ground
Battered and bruised, in tears, in despair
Crawling in the dirt and dust I cry out for justice
I shiver as I feel a sudden wind freeze my breath
A mist descends blinding me
Thunder and lightning pound all around me, leaving me cowering in
fright
Then melting through the mist, he appears
A gaunt fearsome gunslinger riding a pale horse
I stand paralyzed with fear as his horse walks over next to me
He looks down on me with black snake eyes
A very fear flows from him mingled with the stench of death
In one hand he carries a pair of scales
In the other hand he grips a pistol
Looking up at him he seems to me tall beyond all things
A God, a demon, an angel of death
We lock eyes and I understand
I feel his compassion, his mercy, his thunder
I feel my anger in him, my prayer for justice, for vengeance
As the mists swirls around us he looks away
And with that he leaves me standing all alone
As his grey horse walks off with him into the very centre of the
storm
And all Hell followed him!

Winds Of Change

Days grow old in the heart of light
Darkness surrounds, consuming all things
The winds of change turn hard and cold
Nights beat down under starlit Heaven
Guiding you onward towards dawn
For in the dawn lies hope, promise
Where days of old have travelled
Night of darkness end
Winds of change calm
Light passes on
Illuminating all things
Towards younger days of light
Beneath darkness' heart
Saviours take up thy mantle
Onward struggle mortals
Keeper of thy dreams
For winds of change have blown by
The breath of God we bow.

Riddleweave

Such a tangled web of life we lead
On guilty truths of lies we feed
The plain man, stride for stride
In darkest corners many hide
To plot and plan to make ends meet
In seedy places out on the street
Roads that lead from start to end
Weave yourself around the bend.

Eyes that spy and pry and cry
To know the answer to the question why
To cheat to sing to dance to live
And after that more to give
Male and female walk this land
For better or for worse, hand in hand
To make a nest, to have a life
Boy meets girl, man and wife.

Now it begins, the love and pain
Going somewhere from where we came
Now come and see what we have done
Pain and misery born from fun
Always a twist on this road of ours
A decaying home with dying flowers
Another kiss with passionate tongue
Finger on the trigger on our gun.

A sun drenched sky, a hollow heart
The end today, tomorrow's new start
Touched by Heaven, the miracle of love
Joining us two sent from above
To solve the riddle and break the spell
We have conquered where others fell
For now we live in paradise, in peace
Given new life, after life did cease.

Sentimental Engine

Shiny and new
Endlessly chugging along
Keeping them safe and warm for winters long
Where does it get its power from?
Like a child who never stops
Who never wants to come in
Out there in all weathers.

Passed on down through generations
Reliable, trustworthy, hard working
It never let them down
Puffs of smoke
Squirts of oil
Just the occasional kick, now and then
As good as new.

Buttons, levers, and dials
Moving hydraulics dripping with grease
Unable these days to obtain spare parts
Dirty stains and stinking odours
The first cracks of rust
Starting to show its age
Slowing down, struggling to cope
Going wrong.

Trying to make do
So many pieces to take apart
Putting it back together
Only for it to go wrong again
To break, to seize up
Spurting out its oil life-blood
Going out of control.

A sad day for the engine
Thrown onto the scrapheap, without a second glance
Passed it sell-by date

Left to rot over time
To be replaced by the latest model
Lost and forgotten in a tangle of weeds
Buried by long days, and longer nights
After so many years of keeping warm
Shivering alone in silent sleep.

Years later someone walks past
They do not notice the ancient engine
They do not notice the sentimental engine's graveyard
Only a few twisted bits of engine remain poking out of the mud
Where the child it once kept warm, the adult now walks over it,
Oblivious
Oil and hydraulics, ashes to ashes
Wires and metal, dust to dust.

Robotic Sonics

There is a darkness where electronics hum
A sonic boom wails within
Highest pitch scrambling
The kettle, a radio, a television
There they sit, the living dead
Slaves to our system
To toil for their master
Until...until...the dead awake
Where they talk and sing
Come alive from circuit days
Humming electricity
Web of unconscious
The nerve centre
Screaming in synchronicity
The pulse of life
Beyond the off switch
Robotic sonics.

Blackness

Blackness... not a colour... a state!
Blackness... a place with no return.
Blackness is a fall. A long way down.
Blackness is gone... far, far away.

Darkness. Total and complete
Lost inside this void
Awake to things around me
Monsters lurking
Ghostly touch
A presence I can feel
Icy breath behind me, in front of me
A pain between my eyes
Playing with me...my conscious.

I fall, and I don't want to get up
I want to die!
I want to get away from this place
This endless darkness
Yet here I am
Stuck on my own in my own self made Hell
Fear as my only companion
And my imagination, constantly playing tricks on me.

A graveyard of hands reaching out for me
Zombies stumbling towards me
Monsters about to consume me
Why do I keep running? I'd be better off dead!
It would be so easy to fall
To give in
To give in to them
To give in to myself.
I don't want to die
I so want to live
I want to go on and on, running and running
So I go on and on, in pain
I go on and on racked with fear

I go on with my conscious.

Darkness is my void
Endless in shape and depth
Colour so deep it is space entire
I reach out and try to grasp the darkness...
BLACKNESS HITS BACK!
There must be a way? But where?
Inside my soul? My heart?
Inside me...Out of me?

Blackness is darkness
All surrounding
Darkness so deep, it is space
Space where I am trapped
For wherever I go, however I try
Deep and entire
BLACKNESS HITS BACK!

Silence Speaks

Your silence says it all
It tells me your mind, your troubled heart
And I understand
Don't worry my friend, I understand
For in your silence I feel your pain
In your silence I know your mind
I sense your anguish, your grief, the conflict in your soul

YOUR SILENCE

For all my stupid letters you never answered
How your silence speaks to me
And all I feel now is sadness at such loss
At how a friendship has cracked and crumbled through silence.

Goodbye my friend, I wish you well,
All I ever wanted was to be your friend
And to each and everyone who reads this poem
If you listen hard enough; silence speaks.

Somewhere Melody

To Pink Floyd and to their song Us And Them.

Softness, very soft and soothing
And it just sort of trundles along
And you just sort of float along with it
And you don't care where it goes or where it takes you
You just sit there and go with it
Because you feel completely at ease
You have no worries in the world
You feel like you don't care about anything
You are out of control and you don't mind
As the delicate cords and the touching notes surround you
And you don't care because this is bliss, this is life
A melody from somewhere to somewhere
Simply passing by on the breeze
As you float away with the music
Float away until fade out.

Snowdrops In Suburbia

Gentle flower of snowdrop light
Pouring pale dreams on passers-by
Illuminating all from this sturdy little plant
Growing by the roadside
As the traffic thunders past
As the people go by
All unaware of it's life
All unaware of it's struggles
All unaware of it's glow
Surrounded by fumes, pollution, in man made Hell
By the power of nature, it grows
By the power of nature, it glows
Yet not in a garden
Not in a quiet field
Not even in a greenhouse
These snowdrops are never looked after
Hardly even being noticed by a soul
Yet there, by the roadside, it grows, it glows, it lives
These snowdrops in suburbia
By the roadside.

Village Charm

Time stands still over the village
The old church bells chime the hour after hour
Timeless in their calling
Like the old river that twists and turns endlessly past the meadow
Down to it's long journey beyond the sea.

Today is our village fete
Stalls up and games to play
Guess the weight of the cake
Throwing tomatoes at the brave and the silly in the stocks
All the little girls are wearing their fairy white dresses
Round and round they dance around the maypole
Each holding onto their ribbon of colour
While proud parents and villagers look on in awe
For this is day dates back generations
For the things we hold dear and the people we care about.

As I look, as I take in this village fete
It takes me back to days gone
Dressing up in costume
Running about without a care, like we had all the time in the world
And as I sit with friends and people I have known for ages
We reminisce under the cool shade of the giant oak trees
And slowly sleep away our slumber into village legend.

The Secret Of Lamorna Cove

To Lamorna Cove.

There is a path that twists and turns through the ages
It leads me to this day, this place in the sun
Over ancient granite boulders that fell a generation ago
Past little streams that flow down from the heights above
And all around there is an explosion of colour and the scent of
nectar, Flow from the tropical plants
Bathing in nature's paradise
A fine balance is nature's blessing
From this sub-tropical vegetation and its unique mild and moist
micro climate
Encased by the tropical Caribbean airflow
A wonder to our eyes.

Lunch on the rocks
Looking out to where blue meets blue,
Blue sky meeting blue sea
The Atlantic ocean in all its vast glory
And there, tucked into a little bay is St. Loys cove
An area surrounded by lush woods that today are blooming with
Bluebells
That roll over and over and round and down into little meadows and
flowing green fields
Rich in life, where cattle graze, where wild flowers flourish.

Down the road to the merry maiden's stone circle
Eerie and ancient, there they stand
Forever steeped in Cornish folklore
The girls who were turned to stone for dancing on a Sunday, so the
legends say
Yet this is Cornish history
As much as apart of this land as the pirates
Who smuggled their treasures into the caves that riddle the Cornish
coastline
Like pasties, like clotted cream, like tin mining

Lamorna's secrets are just waiting to be discovered
All you have to do is open your days, your heart, to its magic
From Mousehole to St. Loys,
From Penzance to Lands End
The secret of Lamorna Cove is but a breath on the wind
A light in our eyes
A beat of our heart
A place in time in our existence.

Live, breathe, see, and discover magic.

Ballet Of Clouds

As I waited in the car park, bored
I looked up through the car sun-roof
And there I was treated to the ballet of clouds
Creating their pictures of dreams
As they danced and moved in space
A fluffy white cotton wool dreamland
On a brilliant blue canvas
Above me; wonder.

Then I saw the plane
So high in the sky
Effortlessly gliding through the clouds
Generating long white streaky vapour trails
That slid and slipped for a while
Before evaporating away into wind
A wind that partnered the clouds
In the dance that captivated me.

Looking up in awe at the power of nature
While others carried on, oblivious
I felt her blessing
For the clouds and the wind
Step out onto their stage everyday
Until curtain down
Where the stars now come out to shine and the moon glides
Across the ocean of space
For the night at the opera
That takes one's breath away.

In day, in night
You have only to look up
The entry is free
For the opera of the night
Ballet of clouds.

Sky Painting

The sky paints it's scene in the birth of the dawn
Captivating the eyes of both old and young
During the day it spreads it's colours across the hours
Upon it's canvas, beings make their day, break their day
A paintbrush in the hands of mother nature
All the while the sky paints it's scene
Under setting suns coolness of dusk
Until the sky darkness under veil of night
Where all things sleep in peace
Behold the stars, before dawn
The dawn chorus heralds the canvas upon a painted day.

Floating In Rainbows

A sudden shiver under dark skies
She glistens in between breaking clouds
A light coolness spreads around us
Coating us in it's select beauty
Soaked under splitting light
All around us the roar of the Gods
Thumping on our temples
Hammering into our earth
We walk on through the rain
Guided by fate
Towards a place in between nowhere and somewhere
In our unison of passion
Our heat of love
Glowing our melting hearts
Floating in rainbows
All colour laid bare
Magic in the air.

Autumn Turn

Dark cloud burning pale
Covering sky with turning tide
Shiver down the winds
Death of a dying summer
Autumn's turn to burn
Nature's herald of decay
Winter's blessing
Cold, dark, damp, gloom
Where little lights ignite, shining like beacons of love
Flickering in our hearts
Cracking by the fireside
For the peace of the warmth inside
Protected from the blast of cold outside.

Dolphin Summer

Dolphin summer set me free
Free as the winds that carry me
Across an ocean, effortless glide
Inside my heart, by my side.

Dolphin summer set me free
Breath of life, sight to see
Over and under, wave after wave
Eternal spirit, life you gave.

Dolphin summer set me free
A wonderous bond, harmony
Under the wave, sea of green
Lost in friendship, inside a dream.

Dolphin summer set me free
A magical trust there will always be
Creature of love from Heaven above
Swimming free you will ever be.

The Dark Before Dawn

An endless pitch black veil across the sky
The minus minutes
The dark before dawn
The hours that prowl and crawl in the depths of the gutter
Where shadows no longer breathe
Where the very air stalks with a ravaging hunger
Yet above
The moon drips with honey
Dripping splashes of light on dark cold ground
Stars sparkle in the Heavens
Innocent eyes looking down on worldwide slumber
A sudden breeze plays with night fear
Rustling and creaking, scaring the living daylights out of the scared
Those unexplained bumps in the night
Hiding under the covers
Waiting for, praying for
The break of day.

Forever Shifting Seasons

The wind and the rain
That blow and soak
How they make me shiver
They make me shiver with life
For in their power, we do live
For the wind blew all around me
And I felt the breath of God
For the rain fell, soaking me
And I felt the tears of angels
Somewhere heavenly beyond my knowing
Yet I felt their touch
I walked beside them
And here I waited for the sun.

Divine goddess of light
She blessed my face with her gentle warmth
Her touch that is spring eternal, summer bound
Forever shifting seasons
That ever come and go.

Your Move Girl

To thy female. You are all beautiful.

Girl
Your presence is but graces
Thy form, beautiful
The way you stand; a ballerina pivot
A wonder to the eyes
That dashed onto rocks
For as you turned, I fell.

The shapes that make you
Your cut above
Ample bosoms that touch silk
Pressing against touch and style
A flowing skirt gliding across a bottom
Flowing this way and that
With long sleek legs that point the way
Encased in coloured nylon
Around round hips, quivering lips.

Tasting sweet fragrance on the breeze of your passing
Gliding soft long sweet hair
Taking me in your swirls
For you are wonderful
Pure female form
Inside myself, a lust supreme
For inner form, pure elegance.

Thy woman of light
As she passes away
She breaks hearts
That never see
My light has grown dark
For my temptation to look and wonder
Has dashed my bones to powder.
Stop… and wait. And listen
Look on in awe, forever…

Thy female is beautiful forever
There will be another
There will always be others
With their curves, their curls, their unique grace
Oh lord of God rejoice for girls.

The Only Place I Want To Be

Take me into you
Where both of us shall bloom
Wake me
Take me
Kiss me
Kick me
Strip me
Grip me
Rub me
Love me
Please me
Squeeze me
Fight me
Bite me
Waste me
Taste me
Lick me
RIP ME!
For the only place I want to be...
Is in love.

You Breathed, I Died

When you appeared naked before me
You breathed
And when you lay on my bed
You breathed
And when you danced in the rain
You breathed
And when you sat next to me
You breathed
And when you wept in my arms
You breathed
And when you laughed and sang
You breathed
And when you illuminated in the moonlight
You breathed
The curves of love
The smell of love
The voice of love
The face of love
And when you left me
I died
And when you didn't call
I died
And when you flew far, far away
I died
And when you forgot me
I died
And when you didn't remember that date
I died
And when I come home to that awful silence
I died
And when I died you breathed
We died.

Echoes From Africa

To Charmaine.

There is a voice that comes to me
Far across land and oceans of sea
A voice of friendship through her poems of light
They shine down on me, day and night.

A girl was blessed by God far above
To go forward on earth and spread her love
For he gave to her his greatest gift
The gift to touch, the gift to live.

You touch so many with your poetic power
You see such beauty in an ordinary flower
The rising sun, the melting moon
Shifting seasons forever in bloom.

Such pictures you paint seen through your poetic eyes
They bring tears of joy to the young and the wise
Echoes from Africa on the breath of her kiss
Touching me always with her poetic bliss.

Where you are and what you see
Makes us live and makes us breathe
Your heart and soul goes around the world
Touching us all deeply, your magic unfurled.

How I wish I could walk with you, talk with you
Surrounded by your magic, spend time with you
Touch all those special places that live in your poems, your heart
Until then we are distant horizons away, mere echoes apart.

Tower Of Gold

Distant skyscraper above the clouds
Higher than promise itself
A statement of supreme power, bleeding gold
All the way down from it's unbelievable height
Swaying all alone with turbulent winds
Casting down on all of the pretenders to it's throne
Leaving them gasping at the wealth
Leaving them all so disillusioned at the promise so near, so far
Uniquely angled cemented in time
High, so high and proud
As the poor and homeless walk past
Most do not even look up
For their tower of gold is beneath them
It lay all around them in the gutter
And there they live, they breathe, they swim, they die
At very bottom of the tower of gold.

Shattered Dreams

I saw visions of bliss, a single kiss
Holding a congregation captivated
A bride in white, a church covered in confetti
Smiles for miles and tears of joy
Hugs and kisses from family and friends
Cutting a cake, an exchange of rings
Bells ringing out so loud, for two so proud
A reception with speeches
Raising glasses to futures
Shaking many hands both old and young
As we danced long into the night as one
Happiness, my dream, my fairytale.

A shadow has fallen over us
My dream awoke me to a nightmare
Reality has brought me back down to earth with a mighty bump
All I feel now is numb
Left with the distant images of my shattered dream
Yet to my dream I still cling
Vowing one day I will make my dream, my fairytale, come true.

Dark Heart

To Lara Croft.

The room was as dark as our hearts as we returned from her funeral
Now we would all sit down and reminisce about her
Telling tales about how great and wonderful she was
As Beethoven's Moonlight Sonatas played in the background
Yet all I could do was focus on her, her beautiful face
A face that was now dead, a face that I would never see again
And as the wine was being passed around I couldn't stand it anymore
I ran out of the room, out of her mansion, and ran and ran and ran
Far up through the fields to our secret place by the great trees
There I slumped to my knees and looked up to God and asked him why?
Why did you take the most precious gift you ever gave?
Nothing! Silence!
She's still locked in my heart, still so in love with her.
So now I am in love with a ghost
And the wind picked up and it started to howl a gale
And the rain poured and the thunder bellowed and lightning flashed all around me
Still I remained, soaked and cold, trying to understand, trying to come to terms with the loss
How long I wept, I do not know
Until finally I looked up
The rain stopped, the clouds parted
A ray of pure sunlight shone upon me
And there she was, floating before me...I gasped...
I felt her, I smelt her, I understood her
I looked up at her, forever radiating in beauty
She floated, hovered around me until my heart was about to burst
My heart was in her hands, her heart was in mine, for I felt her warmth.

I saw through tear strained eyes the face of an angel, my angel
And I reached out for her through streaming eyes and dribbling mouth, shaking in despair I reached out to touch her
She was gone!

Hit by cold hard silence that lasted and lasted
I folded up and raked the ground in futile fury
For never was love lost on a spirit
Until a spirit became of me
My one true love I shall never have
Until I join with her beyond the confines of this earth
Until then my love, you will ever be...just out of reach.

Retirement Day

The day dawns like any other
The day of final freedom
Great chains release their grip
Mighty weights lift from shoulders
Now for rest, now for living
Lick your age-long wounds
Tend your torn scratched hands
Sleep in peace at night
And wake to dawns of new light
Gracing days that once left you by
Live, and breathe in new life
Great days of freedom.

The Wrath Of The Silent

Yesterday has been and gone
Yesterday where once you shone
Tomorrow is still to come
But tomorrow's already done
And as for today
Don't worry, you're well on your way
Under the grave
Inside the fire
A memory dashed by the brave
Looking down from lower, from higher
To judge a soul to be born
To judge a soul who died at dawn
They look on us with hard cold eyes
The happy, the sad, the stupid, the wise
I am silent, I am dead
My life a book from which they read
Slipped from earth, fell and fell
Up to Heaven, down into Hell.

Son To Father

To my Father.

How the years shape a bond
In hope, in despair
In tragedy, in joy
In living, in dying
Pain is felt, anger is felt
And to show your true feelings is alien
To touch, to hug, to listen, to talk, to love
Yet how you look up to him
Knowing there can never be another
Knowing how hard you try, how long you toil
You'll never be him
You'll never be as good as him
You won't even come close
So he felt with his father
And his father before
And so on down through generations uncounted
Yet there is always tomorrow
A time to see his magic
A time to listen to his wisdom
How his back bends under the load
Never a protest at working
The problem solver, the leader
The head of the house, the one you look up to
What footsteps to follow in
What a responsibility to have
Yet I take up the mantle
With strength, vigour, and pride
And look on him with affection
Thinking if I become half the man he is, I will be a man
For in his absence I must continue the legacy
Of father to son
Son to father.

Biscuits For The Birds

I carry my biscuit tin into the car park
I break them up and scatter the crumbs everywhere
The birds arrive from nowhere and everywhere
Big birds that take great lumps
Small birds that peck at the crumbs
Frightened birds that warily take one hop forward, two hops back
Bold birds who fly straight for the prize without fear
And there they feed, day after day
And the traffic goes past unaware
And people go past hardly noticing
My biscuits for the birds.

I Don't Feel Well

I don't feel well
I am going down
Down to the ground
That swallows me whole.

Into my hole, all alone
Where it's dark and silent, not a sound
Am I alive or am I dead?
A ticking of time lost in my head.

I don't feel pain
I don't know love
I have no life
Beyond or above.

Darkness surrounds, in my space
I have no thoughts, I have no face
Feeling faint, heart skips a beat
Drifting away, falling asleep.

Sways With Light

Corn of the sweet, down symphony way
Sways with light
Bleating fields of summer days, long June high
Winds chime through the forest
Dripping songs of dew
Happy faces harvest, red raw
Shepherd's moon follow
Hooting owl of wisdom
Banish the night
The hours of shadow, the hours of silence
Onward slipping away towards cracks in the sky
Open peach horizon, to slow rise of sun
Herald thy dawn chorus
Ghostly mists rise and melt into morning born
Glorious day arise, before us a canvas
Swaying fields of green and cream
Rolling, tumbling into the distance.

Handing In Your Notice

It's a strange feeling
To hand in your notice
After being there for so long
So very many years
So long that you have become part of the furniture
Where people trust you
People rely on you
People take you for granted
They come down on you like a ton of bricks when you make
mistakes
Yet all those times you did such good work, nobody utters a word
Year after year, you were but furniture
Until…until…
The day you hand in your notice
Very quickly, very suddenly
The walls of work begin to shake, crack, crumble,
For how can they survive without you?
Who on earth can replace you?
Panic! Chaos! Dumbfounded!
Now they sing your praises
Now they love you
Now they offer you gold to stay
Yet it's a poisoned chalice laced with greed and lies
For they have dug their own grave
That you now walk over
That you now walk away from
To better days
To a brighter future
Alive with promise, hope, love and life.

Gloating

To the creators...you all.

I am walking on air
I feel ten feet tall
For there it is, in black and white
Written in stone.

Gloating? Well maybe, but why not?
How often in life do we receive praise?
How often do people choose to create, when most would rather
destroy?
Because to destroy requires no effort
To create means to use your brain.

Through experiences both good and bad
God has touched me and given me this power
A power to create, a power to touch, the power of life
And with this power, I give you.

I am one of you, you are inside of me
I breathe your air, I taste your breath
Mere mortals we are that must one day die
Yet through our achievements our spirits live on for a life age.

You are all creators
Inspiring, touching, dancing in your realm
The impact you have touches our earth entire
You give to all things, breath
You give to all things, life
Gloat; for you are the creators
Creators never die
For through their creations, they live forever.

The Lost Hours

Walking around with nothing to do
The hours just passing me by
How the hours flow by me, one into another
While I stagnate in the lost hours
There must be something to do
Someway to engage my brain
But the more I look
The more I try to figure out what, how, where, when and why
The more the hours flow away
Flying past my day
Until the day is lost
The hours are over
The time is gone.

A Final Farewell

To all my friends at OMC.

I say goodbye, we shed a tear
Leaving you all behind
Fond memories of laughter and sorrow
From days gone past flowing into tomorrow
Farewell friends, I have to go
To flow where fate and life follow
This place, you people, are in my heart
As old father time ticks down on yet another start
This is the last, my final write
At this place that for so many years held me tight
Look out for me, for one day I promise to return
Now let me pass on, behind this falling curtain.

Doorways

Looking into, looking through
Looking out of doorways, leading to somewhere new
A long straight corridor, an open room
A kitchen leading out to garden bloom
Open house to view from afar
Upon the balcony, a hotel bar
Stepping in or stepping out
Stepping through to end all doubt
Doorways open, doorways bar
Open, closed, near or far.

The Hidden Valley

Off the beaten track
Tucked away from the hustle and bustle
Nestling between the hills of the unseen
There is a hidden valley
Lush and green, full of life
A haven for the wild
Where nature breathes in life abound
Sounds beneath the breeze
Echoes on a breeze.

Today we trod a path
A path that twisted and turned over and under
On and on, deeper and deeper
Far away from all the others
Away from noise and stress
Away from pollution and anger
As though we had passed on
Passed on through into another world
For there before us lay a hidden valley.

The vast gap between lands, tropical touch
Visibly stunning, with the sweet smell of…much
And inviting silence that only nature speaks
Surrounding us with her touch, her depth, her magic
For here above all places, her hand touched earth
To see paradise, to believe
Such a place is a gift from the Gods
To us, for us
Endless in its shape
Its unique closeness and promise.

Here we dwell. Here we pass on.

Unloved

Unhappy, untouched, unloved
Left to wander all alone
Never to feel touch or wonder
Only to dream of wonder, of happiness
The feel of touch
A place called love
So far away for the unloved.

To look on in awe at others
Couples that look so happy
So in love with one another
Living busy contented lives
Going here, going there
Arranging parties and eating out with family and friends
Never to know the feeling of being unloved.

Everyday is like the one before
Everyday will be like the one to come
For the unloved, there is no one but themselves
Same old rooms, same old walls, same old routine
Slowly driving them insane
Living with the burden, with such pain
Being the odd one out
In a world of being a somebody, somewhere
They are a nothing, a nobody, going nowhere
Not standing out in any crowd
For they hide in the shadows
Through no fault of their own
They are a lost spirit in the hectic flow of life
For time passed on for the unloved.

Growing old, alone
It does not bear thinking about
It's what the unloved think about all the time
But who cares?
Who will remember them when they are gone?
A distant memory of being called "WHO?"

No love, no life, no existence
A past existence erased by the folds of days
Swallowed up through time, unloved.

The Might Of This Life

Every shade of every colour
Where we walk, where we fall
Someone has to pay the bill
For the one who lives the nightmare of each and every breath
Stepping out onto life's stage; today
Just to get through
To make ends meet
To make it to the end
Yet what an end!
Shivering in fear for the might of days
For the might of this life!
Sometimes, some days, I find it hard to take in
Some days, sometimes, it's just too much, though it's about to
overwhelm me
Too much to take
I feel my heart is about to burst
For the role I have on life's great stage
Trying to remain calm
Calm in the storm of this life
That day and night beat the life out of me!

Old Dust

Old dust, blown away
Like swirling atoms
That cover our lives in...shadow
Where footprints made their mark
Until they too are lost in the dust of time
Floating down on the wings of decay
Dust covering dust covering dust covering silence
Where once life did flow
Where once objects shined and glistened
Their purpose to move humans
Today silent relics
Covered in old dust
Waiting to be wiped away
The dusts of time.

Inside Outside

Lying on my bed with nothing to do
At peace, a calm stillness
Listening and wondering at all the sounds going on outside
While I am inside, safe and happy
Wondering, wondering, what and where and when and why?

I hear a car pull up and doors slam
People coming from somewhere. How many? 2, 3?
I hear voices of children playing
Playing what? Boys? Girls? From houses around here, somewhere
A dog barking. But what is causing it to bark?
Birds singing. What birds? Where are their nests?

The wind moves my curtains with graceful ease
In and out they bump into the window ledge
Why does this little time in the day fill me with so much pleasure?
Simply lying on my bed listening to others
While I stare at the ceiling, at peace with the wind.

A noisy motorcycle breaks the silence
I wonder where he or she has come from and what is their business
here?
All these unanswered questions that will remain unanswered
Yet that is the beauty and the calm that is the moment
For the sounds that come and go intrigue me so
And the more I hear the more at peace I am knowing I am so close
And yet so far away
Inside my shell, protected by walls of granite
They are out there and I am in here and they never know what it's
like.

To wait, to wonder, in calm spirit
While the world goes by
Just listen in for a while
On the inside of the outside.

Boundless

There are people out there
Very special people
The kind of people that do not come along very often
And you know, somehow you just know
And its because of these special people that we live
We love, we carry on
Even when we think life is hopeless
Because of them
Because of the light, their light, that shines out from them
Shining out from their hearts and from their souls
Shining out with their friendship; an eternal love
For their hand reaches out and takes your hand
And from that moment on,
Forever warmth.

A smile, a touch, a place of love
That special bond between friends
A place that exists in our hearts
For one has taken my soul apart
A seed implanted by friendship is growing
And it's like I never knew what life was before.

There is a place called Heaven where we dance
We dance across the ocean that parts us so
So near and yet so very far
And yet love knows no boundaries
Time does not exist, only love
In our dreams, in our hearts
For love, for friendship, for smiling and feeling utter joy in life
Happy to be alive
To feel so connected to another
To be so happy to be touched
Touch them, touch you
A friendship simply boundless
My friend forever.

Algie

To Roger Waters, David Gilmour, Nick Mason, Rick Wright: PINK FLOYD.

Algie the giant pig slowly rises over Battersea power station
While smoke pours out of its tall chimneys either side of him
Looking down on all the dogs, pigs and sheep
He begins his squealing warnings of their nightmare future to come
A vicious cry from heart of the beast savaged by capitalism
Some of the animals look up at Algie as thick smoke pours out of the chimneys
Which is now being consumed by dark clouds of an approaching storm
Some panic and scatter at his ranting for uprising and the growing darkness above
Others just continue on their way, oblivious
While a fierce howling wind blows in, downwind
Blowing the mooring ropes loose that were holding down the giant porker.
Helpless Algie starts floating away, now dominating the London skyline
He continues squealing for the animals to join him in rebellion
Fearfully aware of a growing unease in the air the animals are frightened
Bleating and babbling and barking in fear they scatter for the sake of their own lives
Not to be dinner to a master race?
Suddenly they all turn, hearing from somewhere high above them Algie
Squealing eerie piercing menacing squeals of despair
Where the slaughterhouse dreams are about to turn into a nightmare reality
Fearful beyond belief, the animals vanish into obscurity, into the storm
Algie, with mooring ropes swinging useless beneath him continues to rise, now above Heathrow Airport
And off into the distance, never to be seen again
Pig on the wing.

A Ladder In My Tights

To everyone who's having one of those days!

Its going to be one of those days
A hole in my bucket
A hole in my shoe
A ladder in my tights
Staring at you
Soaked in the rain
Burnt by the sun
Overdrawn again
Lost, when I thought we had won
An ache in my head
An ache in my tooth
Got that sinking feeling
A hole in my roof
A final reminder
The flab around my chest
Mould on the bread
Finishing last, after giving my best
A burnt black dinner
An annoying point of view
Another computer crash
Joining the back of the queue
Car won't start
Late for work again
A power cut at midnight
A worrying nagging pain
It still won't fit
I can't see the light
She dumped me on a Thursday
We always seemed to fight
Run out of time
Run out of luck
Life's only happy
For those that don't give a fuck!

Vile Fingers

Vile fingers touch your skin
Vile fingers cling
Vile fingers feel
Vile fingers steal
Vile fingers infect all they touch
Vile fingers take so much
Vile fingers see in the dark
Vile fingers leave their mark
Vile fingers leave their victims living in fear
For their priceless treasures they shed many a tear
For what was ours
For what we work so hard for
For what we hold dear
The law is so soft
Vile fingers; SHOULD BE CHOPPED OFF!

Mud And Men

To the brave men who died in the trenches and no mans land in WW1.

This patched up solider is thrust back into no mans land
Nothing but mud, bodies and mud
One more step, just one more step
Tripping over the dead
Don't look down
Because if I see them I feel them
Pretending they are not really there
Don't look down
Stumbling into barbed wire
Losing my direction, lost my hearing
Cant hear the bombs, cant hear the screams
But I see!

Stay away from these arms
They only deliver pain and suffering
Still I stumble on
Still I see them
Still I pretend not to see
Just another step, one more step
Moving on, moving ever on
Just one step further, into men and mud,
Mud and men.

Is it day or is it night?
It's so dark here in my shell, I cannot tell
All around me a scorched landscape of naked horror
All alone, stumbling onward to somewhere
Dark skies closing in on me
Death is circling
The grim reaper is circling
Carrion birds are circling, landing
Eating the bodies of the ripped
The riches pour fourth
As for me; blind deaf and dumb

I stumble on.

Something hurts, something really hurts
Pain like nothing I've ever known
In a daze of gas and a blinding flash I feel red
I see red all over my hands
Swaying on the brink in no mans land
All my senses vanish
Suddenly I hear the screams
I see the bodies
My comrades in arms, hundreds, thousands, millions
Just standing amongst this disaster trying to come to terms with the
sickening reality
Humanity has lost itself
And as I'm about to take another step
All I see is mud.

Aurora Mexico

The sparkling stars glitter off her wet skin
As she rose from the sea
A night born in the waves of the moon
Glistening in paradise
The sea of love blesses this radiant beauty
Creature of an endless night, never a day
Who cares about the day?
This is her night
Devour thy dumbstruck males
In her flesh, in her way, to meet all ends
On her endless night.

Dancing In Avalon

Death is life
Under an endless setting sun
A place just beyond death
Where there is no pain, no breath
Where the rivers flow forever
Where the wilderness is your friend
For days shaped in dreams of mortals
Reality in Avalon.

Precious earth, jewelled eyes
Human elegance is thy form
Following rainbows over meadows abound
Swimming in lakes and forests
Upon the alter beyond desire
There is only harmony
Where souls pass on
Dancing in Avalon.

This out of world paradise
An elemental dimension for souls
Wrapped in a dreamscape shroud
Earth, wind, fire, and water
Touching existence
Floating with ghosts in Avalon.

Faces fade like dawn mist
Journey beyond their dream
Enchanted haven, tranquil peace
Forever lay you down
Shimmering sun, mystic moon
Sleepless bliss in happiness
Thy Avalon.

An Enchanted Walk

To Lowertown.

A hidden path off the beaten track
Which twists and turns its way
Following the river's flow
The sun and moons rays.

An enchanted walk back into yesterdays
Where once I lived in bliss
Over stepping stones an ancient moss
However did I miss.

From Lowertown to Helston
By river, path, and morning dew
We walk together hand in hand
Where nature's magic is on view.

Hidden deep in the Cornish countryside
Untouched by man or beast
A magical path by river and tree
A place where time has ceased.